The
A–Z
of
Positivity

THE A–Z OF POSITIVITY

Text by Emily Kearns

An Hachette UK Company
www.hachette.co.uk

Vie Books, an imprint of Summersdale Publishers Ltd
Part of Octopus Publishing Group Limited
Carmelite House
50 Victoria Embankment
LONDON
EC4Y 0DZ
UK

www.summersdale.com

Printed and bound in China

ISBN: 978-1-80007-704-1

Substantial discounts on bulk quantities of Summersdale books are available to corporations, professional associations and other organizations. For details contact general enquiries: telephone: +44 (0) 1243 771107 or email: enquiries@summersdale.com.

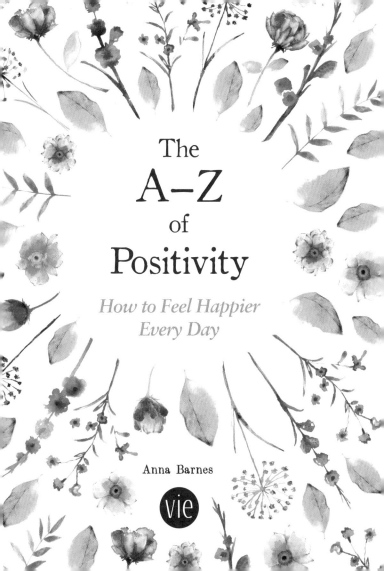

The
A–Z
of
Positivity

*How to Feel Happier
Every Day*

Anna Barnes

vie

Introduction

Practising positivity is about nurturing an optimistic attitude – embracing the present moment as if it were your last. It's about being as kind to yourself as you are to loved ones, investing in your happiness and stepping back from the noise. If you want to attract positivity into your life, then it is absolutely necessary to believe in your abilities and be comfortable with where you are in life, without worrying about what others might have to say. When you live that way – seeing the good in things – no matter what, positivity is sure to flow.

Whether or not positivity is a practice that features in your everyday life, however you go about promoting it, remember there is always room for more joy. Being positive matters, not only to your overall well-being and lifestyle, but to those around you. If you're finding that little by little you need to flip the mood around, then you're in the right place.

In this book, we invite you to make more room for positivity, offering practical advice on how to squeeze optimism into your daily routine. We are all leading increasingly hectic lifestyles and grappling with the task of freeing up space for ourselves. But even small, incremental acts of positivity can go a long way toward lifting your mood and improving your outlook. Change your habits for good, one tip, quote, affirmation and activity at a time – you'll be glad you did when life starts to feel infinitely sunnier.

is for
Affirmations

Positive affirmations are little phrases we repeat to ourselves, the little pledges we make, to actualize the life we always imagined. They are the words we perceive to be true about ourselves and our lives that help put things into perspective, reduce negative thoughts and banish stress.

These uplifting statements need not be a life's work, but a mini celebration of your everyday successes –

small acknowledgements empowering you to hold your head high. We all need a little pick-me-up sometimes, and first thing in the morning is a good time to start. Whether you've just woken up, you're in the bathroom or getting dressed, take a moment to look in the mirror and remind yourself of some of the positive aspects of your life. Or simply give yourself some words of encouragement as you get ready to begin your day.

Positive affirmations can be particularly useful if you have a meeting or presentation, a huge workload or long shift, a job interview, exam or driving test. There are always words you can tell your reflection in the mirror to energize your attitude and put a spring in your step. Try giving these a go:

- I am good at my job and can deal with anything today throws at me
- I am confident, positive and happy – no one can change that
- I can achieve anything I want – I just need to put my mind to it

Make affirmations work for you

Go one step further and write a positive affirmation or two on sticky notes and attach them to your mirror before you go to bed. When you look in the mirror in the morning, these words will help you to feel good about yourself and the day ahead. You could also try writing a handful of positive words about your upcoming day in a notebook as soon as you wake up in the morning; remember to keep them short and sweet, though, for when you repeat them to yourself in the shower, you'll find that some of your affirmations have relevance to your life in general rather than to specific situations. You might find it useful to make a note of these on the lines opposite so that you can come back to them when you need them.

If you have good thoughts they will

shine out of your face like sunbeams

and you will always look lovely.

Roald Dahl

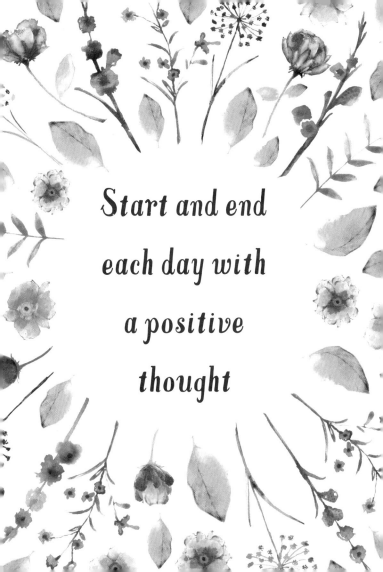

Start and end
each day with
a positive
thought

is for
Believe

As you embark on your journey toward positivity, it's necessary to believe in yourself. That self-belief will carry you through new situations and challenges with a can-do attitude, bringing you one step closer to realizing your day-to-day or lifetime goals. As you set out to get what you really want in life, unleash that positivity within yourself by repeating positive affirmations for building confidence and self-esteem. Your perfect job, partner, pet, hobby, project, or holiday might be around the corner; you just need to go out there and get it. As your confidence takes flight, the resolve to realize your dreams will follow.

Visualization can also help. Take time to sit with your eyes closed and imagine what you want to achieve. Picture the details and let your imagination conjure your goals. Seeing your dreams playing out in your mind can help you on the way toward actualizing them. Jim Carrey is well known for having written himself a $10 million cheque for "acting services rendered" in 1985, dating it ten years in the future. He achieved his goals, so there's no reason why you can't either.

Make a plan

If you'd rather start small and nurture self-belief one step at a time, then try planning for, say, one year ahead. Why not fill out the table below with five things about your life that you are proud of or aspects you would like to change for the better in the coming year? An example under "Work" might be a promotion or a pay rise. While under "Home," you might want to include DIY projects, or maybe your relationship ambitions. And don't forget your successes – they'll surely buoy you up along the way.

	Work	*Home*	*Health*
1			
2			
3			
4			
5			

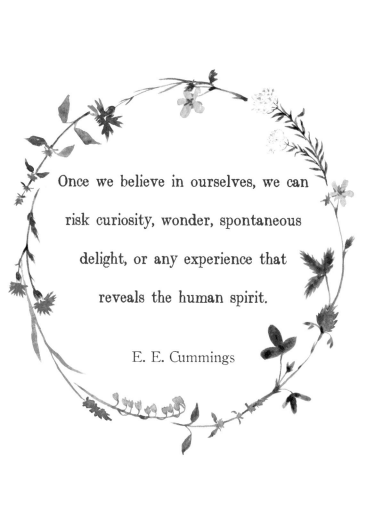

Once we believe in ourselves, we can risk curiosity, wonder, spontaneous delight, or any experience that reveals the human spirit.

E. E. Cummings

is for
Compliment

Compliments can act as mood boosters, giving you a little lift for the rest of the day. As well as pepping up your confidence, a well-placed compliment can even change the way you think about certain things. Consider paying yourself some compliments in the mirror to help you hold your head up high. How about, "You look good today" or "That shirt is definitely a keeper!" Think about how a compliment about the quality of your work from a senior member of staff might put a spring in your step for a week or more, and could even be the push you need to apply for a job or ask for a promotion.

With compliments doing such an excellent job for your self-esteem, remember this will work for others too. Positivity breeds positivity – making a habit of complimenting others will help you on your way to seeing the good in every situation and improving your attitude. Even praising a meal that's been cooked for you with an additional "You know how to get this just right" or "You're such a great cook", can go a long way. And if you like the look of what someone is wearing or how they've styled their hair, then tell them so. Compliments not only bring positivity but can also spark conversations – and what better place to start than on a positive note?

Hand out compliments

Set yourself the goal of paying a handful of compliments each day, both to yourself and to others. Take a moment to think about how you might personalize them. Rather than just commenting on something ("That's such a nice shirt"), try tailoring your compliment ("You really have an eye for a good shirt"). Use the space below to scribble some examples as they come to you.

Be the

reason someone

smiles today

is for
Digital Detox

As the number of digital devices grows, so does our reliance on the virtual realm. Most people now own a smartphone and keep it close by – whatever they are doing. But, whether you're a sucker for social media or addicted to news apps, taking a break from digital devices from time to time can prove beneficial for all sorts of reasons. For one thing, it can improve posture (hunching over a phone for hours can put serious stress on your back and shoulders). It can also increase productivity and strengthen your resolve to exercise. Crucially, a digital detox can simply allow you to live your life. When your eyes are given respite from staring at your phone before bed, you'll likely sleep better too.

Watch your happiness levels soar as you step away from digital doom scrolling and the faux perfect lives that seem to creep into our followed accounts. If cutting yourself off completely is a step too far, then there are various apps that allow you to set limits on how much time you spend on different social media platforms or apps that suck you in and ultimately waste your time. So, take a break or cut down on screen time; you'll absolutely thank yourself when things start to feel more positive.

Take a break from your phone

Try gradually cutting down on your phone use by forming a "time-off" plan. Start by putting your phone on a shelf or in a drawer for an hour. The next day, do the same for two hours, and so on, until you no longer feel a pull toward it and can happily exist screen-free for a few hours at a time.

	Length of time	*How it made you feel*
1 hour		
2 hours		
3 hours		
4 hours		
5 hours		
6 hours		

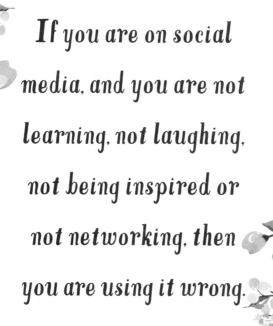

If you are on social media, and you are not learning, not laughing, not being inspired or not networking, then you are using it wrong.

Germany Kent

is for
Exercise

Exercise is the best thing you can do to bring more positivity into your life. That heady mix of neurotransmitters released during heart-pumping aerobic exercise can work absolute wonders for our mental health and well-being. The so-called "runner's high" that can follow intense exercise induces brief feelings of euphoria and a real sense of achievement. When we exercise, our bodies also release cortisol –

a hormone helping us to manage stress. Sounds like a win-win!

If you're new to the world of running there are numerous free apps available designed to help you reach 5K, most using tried-and-tested methods for building stamina over several weeks. Alternatively, take the plunge into cold water with a local wild swimming club. Research has shown that cold-water swimming can boost our immune system, improve circulation, increase libido, and offer a natural high that's incredibly beneficial to our mental health.

If running or swimming isn't for you, how about a dance-fuelled exercise class like Zumba (or something tailored to your music of choice) or a cardio workout to get your blood pumping? This doesn't have to be in person; there's a proliferation of free classes online that you can fit into your routine and really get that positive energy flowing.

Build exercise into your life

Take a moment to think about the activities that induce that feeling of euphoria in you. Now try filling in a wall chart, incorporating those exercises into your weekly schedule. An example of an exercise routine might feature yoga first thing in the morning or before bedtime. It might include a lunchtime run or mindful walk. Maybe even a swim after work. Don't feel you have to do all of these on the same day if the mere thought makes you feel exhausted! Start off slowly and be flexible. Just make sure you stick with it. Remember, as your stamina builds, so will your positive outlook.

If you're the kind of person who needs a gym membership or regular class to keep you motivated, then take that route. Ensure you're reaping the benefits by monitoring your progress and making a note of how

each exercise session makes you feel. Starting a plan which features various types of exercise and tracks your mood may well be one of the best things you ever do for your health all round.

	Monday	Tuesday	Wednesday	Thursday	Friday
Morning					
Afternoon					
Evening					

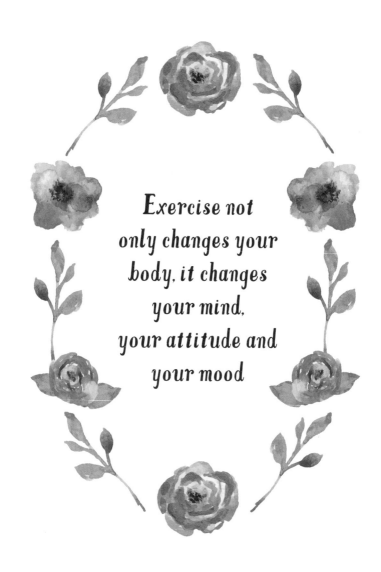

Exercise not only changes your body, it changes your mind, your attitude and your mood

The hardest thing about exercise

is to start doing it. Once you

are doing exercise regularly, the

hardest thing is to stop it.

Erin Gray

is for
Focus

Modern life is full of distractions. We all try to juggle numerous aspects of our lives, jumping from one thing to the next, often spreading ourselves too thin to get everything done, seldom giving our complete focus to one task at a time. On top of that, technological distractions buzz and beep at us and pull us out of our concentration.

If you find yourself easily distracted, prone to daydreaming or picking up your phone too often to check for notifications, fear not: there are ways to improve your focus and gain a more positive mindset. The key is to banish bad habits and develop good ones. Remove distractions by taking yourself into a calm space where you won't be bothered and will instead be able to give each task your full attention. Try to pull your thoughts back to the moment if you find they wander. The more you do this, the more you'll find it easier to focus. Forget multitasking and instead give your all to the task of the moment. If you start to feel frazzled, take a short break and focus on something else – but only for a short period of time – then head back to what you were doing and your focus should be renewed.

One thing at a time

Name one priority task you need to complete below.
Now list what's needed for you to complete it.

Focus and simplicity... once you get

there you can move mountains.

Steve Jobs

is for
Gratitude

Practising gratitude is widely thought to be helpful in achieving greater positivity and happiness. By taking time to reflect on the things we value most in life and feeling thankful for them, we shift our focus to a more positive place and push the negative thoughts to one side.

It's easy to practise gratitude every day. You might find the best time is to take a moment before you go to sleep to reflect on the day and think of the things for which you feel thankful. You might want to focus your gratitude on friends, family, work, or health – but don't forget the many day-to-day things we often take for granted, such as food and shelter, clean water and a safe living environment.

When it comes to practising gratitude, you are in charge. If you want to spend time feeling thankful for finding your glasses or keys when you thought you'd lost them or for a delicious slice of chocolate cake that you have just inhaled, that's up to you.

Other ways to practise gratitude could involve telling the people in your life that you are thankful for their presence and spending quality time with them. You might want to volunteer, to give something back to your local community and help others. Or you could keep a gratitude journal (see next task), referring to your thoughts of thanks whenever you feel negativity creeping in.

Keep a gratitude journal

Let the positivity flow by keeping a gratitude journal – something you can return to whenever you feel the need to count your blessings. Just a couple of lines will suffice. Use the space below to write down what you feel thankful for today.

Gratitude is the fairest blossom

which springs from the soul.

Henry Ward Beecher

is for
Hydrate

Drinking too little water can leave our energy levels depleted and our brain function impaired, leading to headaches and fatigue. It's no wonder water is vital to our health in so many ways. For example, water helps lubricate our joints, flush out bodily waste, regulate body temperature, maintain healthy blood pressure and keep the kidneys functioning properly.

Guidance on how much we should drink each day varies around the world, with climate being an important factor, but a good amount to aim for is approximately 2 litres over a 24-hour period. Remember that on particularly hot days or when exercising, you'll need to consume more. Don't forget that other drinks contain water, as do ice lollies and soups, among other foods – all of which count toward your daily total.

As we work toward developing a more positive mindset, remember that water is necessary for our physical and our mental health. Make consuming enough water a priority to function at your very best. And while you're drinking, take time to practise gratitude and remember how lucky we are to have access to clean water when much of the world is not so lucky. Perhaps you could even jot this down in your gratitude journal (see page 36).

Jazz up your water

If you're not the world's biggest fan of plain water, fear not – there are plenty of ways to jazz up your daily dose. Try adding a selection of the following ingredients to create something a little more interesting:

- Ginger, lemon, orange and/or cucumber (sliced or spiralized)
- Raspberries and/or pineapple (crushed)
- Mint leaves (bruised)
- Lime wedges (squeezed)

In time and with water,

everything changes.

Leonardo da Vinci

is for
Inspiration

Surrounding ourselves with inspiration can have a profound effect on how we live our lives. You might find inspiration in friends or family members, perhaps work colleagues or senior members of staff within your organization. Maybe you recently found you were moved by a piece of art or music. Perhaps you find a public figure truly inspiring, an author whose words speak to you in a way that others do not. You may well be hankering after a dream job and admire someone who has already achieved this.

Having an inspiring presence in our lives can move us from apathy to possibility, transforming the way we judge our own abilities. Sometimes seeing others succeed serves as a catalyst for change – a light bulb moment when we realize it's about time we stepped outside our comfort zone. That motivational trigger can just be the push we need to take practical steps toward achieving our goals, toward feeling more positive about the life we're living.

If something inspires you, hold on to it, pursue it. If a piece of art or music, or perhaps a book, has moved you and occupied your thoughts since, seek out more from those artists or authors and think about why they moved you so. Feeling inspired about things puts a spring in your step, which will help to spread positivity through your life.

Set your goals

Choose a goal (perhaps you want to run that marathon or change your career) and create a (digital) mood board with tips, inspirational quotes and ideas on how to make your dream a reality. Alternatively, use sticky notes to leave little reminders of your greatness all over the place for you to catch sight of throughout the day.

Surround
yourself
with calm and
positivity

is for
Joy

Look for joy in the everyday things and happiness and positivity will likely follow. Perhaps the sound of the rain on the roof brings you a sense of joy through your contentment at being safe in the warm and dry. Or perhaps a delicious meal (especially after exercising) or a hot cup of tea in a moment of calm and quiet might do the trick. Or maybe just watching the world go by will do it for you.

Socializing with friends and family might be what causes your cup of joy to "run over" – making time for those who know us best and with whom we can truly be ourselves (perhaps even our silly selves) is key to unlocking more joy.

And don't forget to be playful – as adults we so often do. Try to remember your youthful spirit (we all have one) and let it come out to play when you need a break from the grind of daily life. Do something out of the ordinary and challenge yourself to have fun with it – whether that's dancing when nobody's watching, singing in the shower, jumping in puddles, eating chocolate cake in the bath, building sandcastles, tossing a Frisbee, or riding the Waltzer ride at your local fairground. Remembering to enjoy yourself is one of the most important things in life and will improve your outlook no end.

Bring on the joy

Set a timer for five minutes and write down (in the space below) everything in life that brings you joy. This activity can only end one way: on a high.

Joy is what happens to us when
we allow ourselves to recognize
how good things really are.

Marianne Williamson

is for
Kindness

The world would be a much more positive place if we all were kinder to one another. Vowing always to be considerate of others, striving to treat everyone as you would like to be treated yourself, is a good starting point. But there's always more to give.

Go further by volunteering within your local community (at a food bank, for example) or spending time with the lonely. An elderly person with limited mobility might really be buoyed by a social visit, even if for a quick chat over a coffee. When for whatever reason someone lacks the ability to read or sing, doing just that might take them (and you) to a more positive plane of existence.

Alternatively, you could put your transferable skills to good use by, for instance say, tutoring a child who's struggling or babysitting for friends in need of a break. The very definition of kindness is "being friendly, generous and considerate" without expecting anything in return. However, it's okay to admit that kindness reaps its own rewards: being kind makes us feel good and spreading it will only bring more positivity into our lives. There are a million ways to demonstrate kindness – perhaps it's time to up your game?

Perform a random act of kindness

Carry out a random act of kindness this week by paying someone an unexpected compliment. It's okay to start small, following up a smile at a stranger in the street with a compliment on their choice of sunglasses, for example. Once you get into the mindset, random acts of kindness will come to you. You could write some ideas for compliments below to get some practice. Before you know it, you'll be dishing out compliments to strangers all the time, helping to make the world a sunnier place.

One small act of kindness

can go a long way

is for
Laughter

It's official: laughter is good for your health. And on so many levels – physical and mental. As the old saying goes, "laughter is the best medicine" thanks to the relaxing effect it has on the body. Research shows that we breathe better after a good bout of laughter (much like after aerobic exercise), letting in more oxygen and increasing our heart rate, which in some cases may offer an antidote to stress and high blood pressure – a major risk factor in heart disease and stroke.

Think about how you feel when you spend time with friends or family who share your sense of humour, or the last time you watched live comedy. Unless the experience was awful, you probably left on a bit of a high, right? That's because laughing together promotes positive feelings. Laughter therapy has been found to reduce anxiety and improve optimism and self-esteem, maybe even act as a natural antidepressant. These findings have led to the introduction of a laughter-based yoga practice, whereby participants use laughter as a form of bodily exercise, inducing real and contagious laughter.

Have a laugh

Try laughter therapy for yourself. You can do this alone but doing it with friends and in good company can lead to a lot of very natural laughter – only adding to the benefits of the practice.

Have a go at one of these:

- Hold your breath and burst out laughing when you can't hold it any longer.
- Introduce yourself to the group (or mirror) and laugh while you do so.
- Do some laughter counting by building up from "ha" to "haha" to "hahaha", etc., until you are laughing continuously.

- In a group, hold hands in a circle. Run towards each other and burst out laughing when you reach the centre.
- Smile, then giggle, start to laugh slowly and quietly, gradually increasing in tempo and volume until you burst into natural laughter.

We all laugh
in the same
language

*Always laugh when you can. **It is** cheap medicine.*

Lord Byron

is for
Music

Music is known for having an impact on our emotions, with certain pieces of music taking our thoughts to places of joy, sadness, contemplation and stirring memories in a unique and immediate way. As well as affecting our emotions, music has been found to reduce stress and anxiety, even the perceived intensity of pain, by aiding blood flow, which in turn improves heart health.

If music isn't already a big part of your life, then try to let more in. Consider taking yourself off to watch some live music; you might find plenty of free gigs right on your doorstep and feel your mood lift as the band begins to play. You could have a go at compiling a playlist of your favourite upbeat songs (the ones that make you bright-eyed and in the mood for dancing), so you'll always have something to listen to whenever you need a pick-me-up. There's an abundance of new music out there, probably too much to ever have the time to listen to, so ask friends for digital mixtapes or playlists for inspiration or surprise. Put the radio on when you're doing the washing up or getting ready. Just let those positive vibes flow.

Dance in your kitchen

Why not treat yourself to a kitchen disco, the next time you're cooking dinner? Simply ramp up your favourite dance-floor-filling playlist, crack out your best moves and sing at the top of your voice. A burst of uninhibited fun is bound to send your positivity levels soaring.

One good thing about music:

when it hits you, you feel no pain.

Bob Marley

is for
Nature

The benefits of lush green spaces are boundless. As we fill our lungs with fresh air, we even breathe differently. Getting out and about in nature forces us to be more active. Our physical health improves as a result, and our confidence and self-esteem switches into a higher gear. Take the time to visit a green space near to where you live. While you're there, perhaps try practising gratitude by feeling thankful for what nature has to offer.

Try mindfulness meditation at the same time, simply by looking around and listening to the sounds of nature: a breeze through the tree branches, birds calling, a rustle in the undergrowth. If you feel your mind wandering, bring it back into the present moment, and concentrate on the immediacy of the sounds all around you.

Being in natural surroundings, listening to the sounds we experience in those spaces, can instil a sense of calm. This can give us space to think, away from the distractions of home. Natural light is also incredibly beneficial, among other things, for boosting vitamin D, warding off seasonal depression and improving sleep. You might also want to have a go at tending to whatever outside space you might have around your home; caring for plants and flowers can help us learn to better care for ourselves. Immersing yourself in nature will be such a positive leap in the right direction you'll find that before you know it you're hooked and eager to get outside whenever you can.

Explore local green spaces

Make a list of your favourite green spaces and places, be they community woodlands, parks and gardens, wetlands, salt marshes – anywhere that will see you outdoors and immersed in nature. Return to this list when you feel uninspired. The very act of writing them down will likely plant seeds in your mind, prompting you to recall them time and again for that natural high.

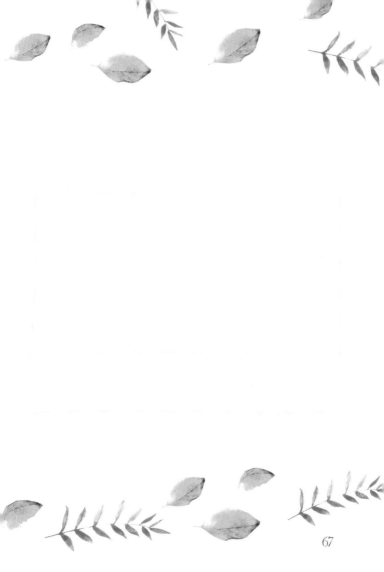

Let nature soothe

your soul

Look deep into nature, and

then you will understand

everything better.

Albert Einstein

is for
Organize

Everyone knows cleaning and clearing out clutter can help to decrease stress and anxiety. If you're living in a chaotic environment, surrounded by a mess, it's not uncommon to feel like you're losing control. Taking back that grip on reality can make you feel empowered, relaxed and infinitely more positive.

Sorting out your living space and letting go of things you no longer use or need can feel overwhelming, but it doesn't need to be a daunting task. If it's something you're putting off, simply tackle it one step at a time. Set yourself a small task each day, sorting out a drawer, cupboard, or corner of a room. Before you know it, you'll have made real progress.

You might even find that you can make a little money by selling the things you no longer need – your trash could be someone else's treasure. Rather than throwing away the items you deem unsellable, think about leaving them outside your home with a note inviting passers-by to help themselves. Or advertise them for free via an online platform. The ultimate goal is to keep these things out of landfill, and rehoming and repurposing where possible, allowing you to pursue a more positive life.

Get organized

Try some of these organizing tips to bring some positivity and balance into your life:

- Arrange books by colour – this isn't for everyone, but it can have a joyous effect on a room.
- Organize your pasta, dried pulses and other kitchen staples into glass jars to create a pleasing aesthetic look.
- Buy some clothes hanger connectors to double or triple your wardrobe hanging space.
- Streamline storage, making sure everything in your home has a place to live.

Have nothing in your houses that

you do not know to be useful,

or believe to be beautiful.

William Morris

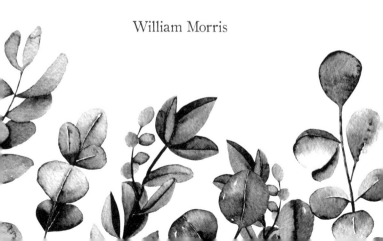

is for
Positive
Mental Attitude

PMA is a life philosophy whereby you try your hardest to see the good in every situation and live with an optimistic attitude. It's about looking at life with a glass-half-full mentality, rather than focusing on the negatives. It's also about taking a positive situation and finding yet more joy within it. When you look for the smaller joyful elements, your cup will overflow.

Learning to live this way is easier than you think. Try to start each day with a positive thought or action. Perhaps exercise is a good way to kick things off – a run, swim or yoga session can do wonders to start your day with a positive mindset. Maybe practising gratitude first thing in the morning will put you on the right track.

Filling your life with the people who make you feel good, who make your life better (rather than those who leave you feeling drained and hollow) is a step in the right direction. Research has found that positive thinking is linked with improved cognitive performance; those who approach life with a more optimistic outlook often take chances where others might talk themselves out of things. If you believe you can do something, then do it!

Use the space below to write down everything that features in your calendar over the next week or month. Now write something positive next to each activity – whether it's a work meeting, a social event, or a health appointment. Exercises like this will help you start seeing the positives in every situation.

A positive mental attitude is

the right mental attitude.

Napoleon Hill

is for
Quiet

While chaos can sometimes be joyful and there are many a noise that bring us great happiness – like children laughing and squealing outside, groups of friends excitedly chatting after time apart, or the bustle of a summer carnival – we should all make room for a little quiet in our lives. Stillness and quiet afford us a chance for contemplation when our minds feel busy and it can be difficult to think.

Find some time to embrace the stillness of a quieter place to appreciate the calm it can bring. Sit in a quiet space for several minutes. Switch off your thoughts. If you feel your brain buzzing, concentrate on the sound of your breathing and think about your breath going in and out, as it inflates your lungs and brings you life.

If life generally can be quite noisy – either at home or work – it can be useful to practise filtering out the noise so that you can think more clearly. Learning to banish unwanted sounds in this way can help to lower stress levels that build up as noises layer over each other. When we're tired or stressed, we're particularly sensitive to certain sounds. Switch off any noisy machines and unlock your best internal sound filter. Close your eyes and enjoy the beauty of the quiet space around you.

Breathe deeply

Try this simple breathing exercise to find a moment of calm and positivity in your quiet space.

- Put one hand on your chest and the other on your stomach.
- Breathe in deeply through your nose for a count of four seconds and hold the breath for another four seconds.
- Breathe out through your mouth slowly over another four seconds.
- Repeat around ten times or until you begin to feel more relaxed and positive.

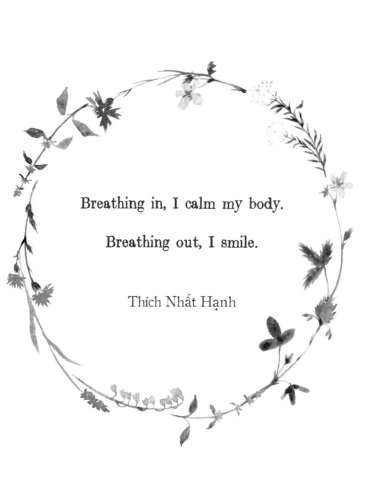

Breathing in, I calm my body.

Breathing out, I smile.

Thích Nhất Hạnh

is for
Recharge

It's important to take regular breaks from work to recharge your internal batteries, keep your positivity levels topped up and avoid getting too close to burnout. It can also be hugely beneficial to have a break from your daily routine and give yourself a bit of a reset. Both your body and your mind will thank you.

You might find a good walk or run in the middle of your day helps to break things up, or at the end of your working day it might help you wind down into your free time. Morning or evening exercise – whether that's a walk, run, workout, swim, yoga, or exercise class – can also help bring you energy after a long day at work.

Holidays are vital too. If you'd rather not go abroad, then plan a staycation, aiming for an entire week off. Fill your days with new activities and visits to new places, making time to see friends and family, and treating yourself to hearty food. The benefits of time off work are vital – you'll feel rejuvenated and refreshed and more grateful than ever before.

While you're at it, why not plan a quarterly guilt-free "do nothing" day? Avoid making plans so that, on this special day, you can see where life takes you. Whatever you decide to do with that time, (heading out, having a lie-in, reading a book, etc.), remember, it's your day, so no guilt!

Puzzles for positivity

If you find it hard to take a break, this page is for you. Sit down somewhere quiet and search for the positive words in the wordsearch opposite. Taking five minutes out of your day to give your mind a rest might be just what you need.

N	G	J	L	Z	U	H	H	T	D	T	P
A	O	E	O	V	G	Z	P	A	H	H	E
H	B	P	Q	Y	S	B	S	G	P	G	A
P	O	Y	E	Q	S	A	I	H	R	P	E
S	S	P	N	B	L	R	I	A	I	D	Y
U	S	A	E	J	B	T	H	Z	U	P	H
N	M	U	R	P	K	C	V	T	L	M	C
S	I	P	G	P	E	N	I	Q	W	A	P
H	L	L	Y	R	N	T	O	X	R	Q	B
I	E	I	J	S	A	R	Q	B	C	D	Z
N	C	F	S	R	I	U	P	B	E	A	T
E	F	T	G	A	Z	W	D	E	A	A	B

Bright	Hope	Smile
Energy	Joy	Sunshine
Gratitude	PMA	Upbeat
Happy	Recharge	Uplift

Remember to rest

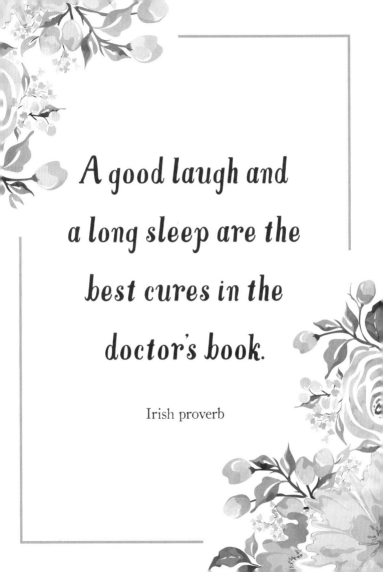

A good laugh and
a long sleep are the
best cures in the
doctor's book.

Irish proverb

is for
Spontaneity

Open yourself up to spontaneity and you will thank yourself for the rewards it delivers. Not only will being spontaneous bring more positivity into your life, but you will likely experience countless things you otherwise would not have experienced and find yourself with a renewed zest for the beauty of the day-to-day. While structure in life can bring comfort and security, sometimes it can become rigid and we need to loosen things up a bit.

Start by agreeing to say "yes" to everything. You could try this as an experiment for a day or a week and see where it takes you. Once the experiment is over you'll find yourself agreeing to more than you did before.

Take a look at your daily routine and habits and try and change things around. Do you walk or drive the same way to work every day? Try taking a different route to keep things interesting. Do you always order the same thing when you go out to eat? Go wild and try something else.

Those who invite spontaneity into their lives are likely to be flexible and relaxed, happier and less stressed. They are often more creative and better at forming bonds with others. The positives here really add up.

Embrace spontaneity

If life feels too busy to say yes to everything, try being spontaneous – on your lunchbreak, for example. Set off with no plan as to where you're going or what you're going to do. Let your feet take you on a micro-adventure and see where you end up. Add new activities to your routine and – as long as you enjoy them – you will feel your mindset shifting.

Why not seize the pleasure at once?

How often is happiness destroyed

by preparation, foolish preparation!

Jane Austen

is for
Thrill

It's unlikely that anyone has ever described their day as "thrilling" without a positive spring in their step. What is it that gives you that thrill? That feeling of immense pleasure that makes your soul sing.

Perhaps you love riding roller coasters? Plan to spend a day at a theme park soon. Maybe you'd rather watch horror films through the comfort of an old blanket. If you find crochet truly thrilling (everyone has a comfort zone), then find a new project to get your teeth into (and then maybe sign up for a skydive). If extreme sports, like skiing or snowboarding, are your bag but it's off season, then watch some old videos of previous trips with friends to immerse yourself in your shared passion while the activity itself is out of reach. Thrilling activities can cause a rush of adrenaline, bringing about feelings of euphoria and helping to lift our mood immeasurably.

Find your thrill

Use the space below to list the activities you find truly thrilling. Don't be shy – this is for your eyes only. Return to this when you need a boost.

Adrenaline is my drug of choice.

Kate Angell

is for
Uplift

What makes you feel uplifted? What lifts your mood to the next level to help you feel more cheerful and positive? Start with the little things. What makes you feel good in life? Maybe it's a big night out or a bear hug from an old friend, partner or family member? Perhaps you dream about travel and adventure, meeting new people and visiting interesting places? Dream bigger.

Can you think of anything you used to really enjoy doing that you don't have time for any more? Go back to it! Even if you only have the time to return to your favourite uplifting activity in a smaller capacity, you will be grateful you did, and you'll wonder why you ever stopped. Being available for things that elevate our mood is therapeutic; it helps to banish stress and boost positivity. Whatever it is that makes you feel uplifted, invite more of it into your life.

Write a happy list

Use the space below to write your "happy list". What helps you to feel uplifted? It could be anything: people, animals, activities, places, moments, weather – whatever comes to mind.

The sky's the limit

is for
Vegetables

Yes, vegetables! There are plenty out there that can help boost positivity. Folate-rich vegetables such as spinach, broccoli, kale and artichokes all help with the production of dopamine – one of our "happy" hormones. To promote positivity, make sure you're eating plenty of these regularly. If you find it hard to incorporate them all into your diet, then make the smoothie on page 102 a regular fixture and give yourself a boost that way.

Eating a "rainbow" of vegetables (and fruit) will set you up with the full complement of vitamins, minerals and antioxidants these staples have to offer. It's widely recommended we consume at least five portions of fruit and veg a day, which'll be relatively easy for those following a plant-based diet, potentially trickier for those who don't. Look for ways to add fruit and veg into your daily routine via smoothies and juices, snacks and side dishes. If you're not much of a veggie eater, introduce a new one to your diet each week and try out some new dishes or incorporate it into old favourites.

Whip up a green smoothie

Try this delicious smoothie to get your day off to a flying start. Place all ingredients in a blender and serve!

Serves one

Ingredients:
- 1 orange, juiced
- Handful of strawberries
- Large handful of spinach or two small frozen portions
- 1 stick of celery
- 5 cm cucumber
- Half an avocado
- 75 ml (3.5 fl oz) milk or plant-based alternative

Eat good,

feel good

is for
Water

This time it's less about drinking water, but more about immersing yourself in it. Hot or cold, there are many benefits to be had in your quest for a more positive mindset. Remember, if you're heading to a nearby lake or seashore, stay swim-safe by checking out local recommended spots, taking a friend, or joining a wild swimming group.

Swimming generally is a great form of exercise for getting your heart rate going without putting stress on your body. It's also great for giving your limbs a good old stretch, for toning your muscles and for building strength.

Getting your swim on in some cold water also has immune-system-boosting qualities – doing wonders for your circulation, and even your libido. Regular cold-water swimmers claim to experience a natural high that lasts for the rest of the day. They often feel the urge to get in the sea as often as they can. A steaming-hot bath at the end of a cold day will also work miracles for your well-being, relaxing your muscles and improving circulation. There are also claims it helps to lower our blood pressure and does wonders to clear up and moisturize our skin, depending on what you're soaking in. Relax with a book and escape to a happy place.

Set a swim challenge

Set yourself a challenge to build up your swimming strength. Start with a manageable number of lengths and work up from there, perhaps adding two to four laps each time for stamina. Don't worry about starting low; this is how we build strength and improve technique. Use the table opposite to record how you feel after each session.

	No. of laps	How you feel
Week 1		
Week 2		
Week 3		
Week 4		
Week 5		
Week 6		
Week 7		
Week 8		
Week 9		
Week 10		

Natural water has always held

the magical power to cure.

Roger Deakin

Let all your worries

float away

is for
X-factor

Your X-factor is your strongest quality or skill. Take your talent and nurture it. You might be excellent at baking or cooking, or maybe you're creative when it comes to crafting. Perhaps you used to play an instrument, paint or draw, but don't do much of that anymore. Go back to it, practise, relish the joy it'll bring not only through enjoyment of the act itself, but through the realization that you're getting better the more you do it.

If singing's your thing, start by singing at home when no one else is around and work up to joining a choir or singing group. Maybe you're brilliant at DIY and could help clueless friends and family when all your jobs have been done. As well as showing off your talents, you'll gain a sense of joy and fulfilment knowing you're helping others.

We all have something we're good at, but sometimes we find it hard to admit even to ourselves that we excel in a certain area. By focusing on what it is that we can do well, we excel in our talent and build our confidence – ultimately inviting positivity in to stay for good.

Try something new

Why not try something you never thought you were good at before? Borrow an instrument from a friend or ask an arty pal if you can paint or draw with them. Unleash your potential and have fun with it.

True happiness involves the full

use of one's power and talents.

John W. Gardner

is for
Yoga

Yoga is a wonderful form of exercise that is highly beneficial for body, mind and spirit. It not only improves strength, flexibility and balance, but it also helps tone muscles, boost blood flow, reduce stress and promote relaxation. On top of that, yoga can help you sleep better – need any more reasons? As a practice, it is also excellent for mild aches and pains, stiff shoulders and posture – complaints that are rife in our modern world of desk-bound working.

Schools of thought on yoga vary from the very energetic to the incredibly gentle and thoughtful, so you will easily find something that suits you. Try hot yoga if you're feeling brave and up for a sweat; opt for Hatha or Ashtanga if you're looking to lower the temperature and stretch out your body alongside breathwork; or Vinyasa – where you move from one pose directly into the next – if you're in the mood for something more energetic. With so many physical classes you can join in a variety of styles and abilities; there really is no excuse, especially when you look at the number of free yoga videos on the internet. If you can't find a class in your area, search online.

Tree pose

This classic yoga pose will help you to feel centred, build strength and practise balance. Stand tall, with your feet together and arms at your sides. Press your toes into the mat. With hands on hips, lift your right leg, bend it at the knee and bring your right foot to rest on the inside of your left leg. Softly gaze at a spot on the floor to help you balance. Depending on how steady you feel, you can have your right foot resting on your left ankle, left lower leg, or left thigh, but avoid resting your foot at your knee. Bring your hands together in prayer position and hold the posture for several breaths before swapping to the other side.

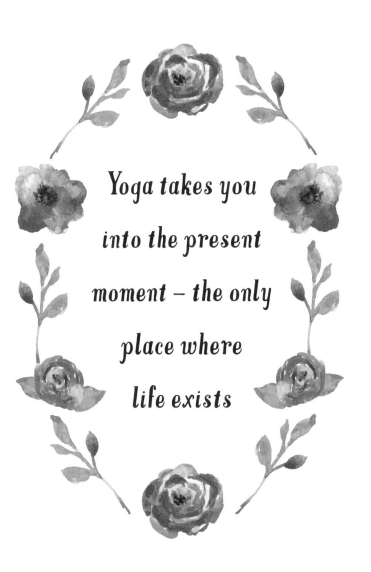

Yoga takes you

into the present

moment – the only

place where

life exists

is for
Zen

Zen is a tradition originating in Buddhism which seeks to free the mind from words and logic in a quest to look deep into the self. In a nutshell, Zen is all about relaxing into meditation and enjoying peace, quiet and relaxation.

Meditation – a technique where we are quiet and still, and train our focus to our thoughts and feelings, observing them from a heightened state of awareness –

can help you gain a new perspective in times of stress. It can also help you to focus on the present, reduce negative emotions and increase your patience, imagination and creativity. You'll find that meditating, when performed regularly, improves the quality and length of sleep, and can reduce feelings of anxiety and depression.

While it can be incredibly beneficial to work meditation into your daily routine – even if only for five to ten minutes a day – it can be useful to call on it when stressful situations arise, whether that's at work or home, after a long, busy commute or simply after watching the news. You might find getting out of bed to meditate in the morning is the best time for you, or perhaps just before you go to bed to get you into the zone for a deep sleep. Whatever time suits you best, just try to build it into your routine so the habit sticks.

Take time to meditate

Try this simple meditation to get you started:

- Sit down somewhere quiet and get comfortable – cross-legged on a cushion on the floor is ideal, but on a chair will do just fine.
- Set a timer for five to ten minutes.
- Close your eyes or soften your gaze.
- Notice your body, think about how it feels. Work your way through it starting with the top of your head, and slowly moving your attention down to your toes.
- Follow your breath as it goes in and out and notice the sensation.
- If your mind wanders, bring it back by focusing on your breathing.
- When your time is up, think about how your body feels. How about your emotions?

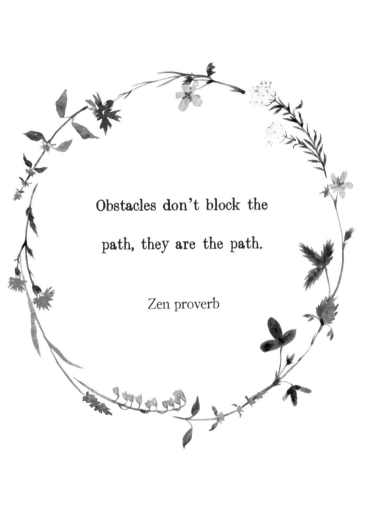

Obstacles don't block the

path, they are the path.

Zen proverb

Conclusion

You must be oozing positivity by now! Here's hoping this book has set you on a path toward a happier and more fulfilled life. If you take these tips on board and incorporate them into your daily routine, there's no reason why you can't edge over to the sunnier side of the street. However you go about forging a more positive mindset – from giving thanks daily for all that surrounds you, to spreading joy and kindness, to decluttering your home – just remember to hold onto the truth that there's nothing stopping you from harnessing the power of positivity.

Bringing more optimism into your day-to-day life by adopting a positive mental attitude – finding the joyful elements in every situation, no matter how small – will help you to bring about positive change permanently. Embrace every small triumph and hold on tight. Be true to yourself and, above all, really feel all your feelings.

Be bold and open the door to the sun, letting its feel-good rays nurture your inner confidence to go out there and live life to the fullest. What are you waiting for? Be the change you want to see by making the world a more positive place.

Make your own destiny – don't wait for it to come to you

Write it on your heart that every

day is the best day in the year.

Ralph Waldo Emerson

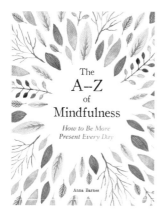

The A–Z of Mindfulness

Anna Barnes

ISBN: 978-1-78783-273-2

Hardback

Squeeze every drop out of each moment and live life to the full by discovering the art of mindfulness. Learn new ways to connect with yourself and the world around you and reignite a sense of wonder in the everyday with this practical ABC of illustrated tips for mindful living.

The A–Z of Wellbeing

Anna Barnes

ISBN: 978-1-80007-705-8

Hardback

The things that add up to happier life don't have to be complicated. Whether you choose to dance and sing, give yoga a go or tap into the power of quietude and kindness, this charming A–Z guide will help you find your perfect path towards a greater sense of wellbeing.

Image credits

If you're interested in finding out more about our books, find us on Facebook at **Summersdale Publishers**, on Twitter at **@Summersdale** and on Instagram at **@Summersdalebooks** and get in touch. We'd love to hear from you!.

www.summersdale.com